The Tale of the Lancashire Witches

by

Arthur Douglas

Photographs by Stuart Mason

The text in this publication is scripted in such a way that it may be spoken direct onto tape and used in cassette form, an application that might, hopefully, find its place in schools and as an aid to tourism. It is pointed out, however, that the words, style and form herein applied are the subject of copyright and must not be so reproduced without the consent in writing of the publishers.

Published by Countryside Publications Limited, School Lane, Brinscall, Chorley, Lancashire.

Printed by Tamley-Reed Limited.

ISBN 0 86157 001 4

Contents

FULLY ILLUSTRATED

Alizon Device encounters John Law on the road to Colne.

Part One: The Pendle Brood

Episode One

The road to Colne

It is the eighteenth day of March in the year sixteen-hundred and twelve, and Alizon Device is in the vicinity of Colne on a begging expedition to Trawden when she encounters John Law, a petty chapman from Halifax, and asks him for some pins. When the pedlar refuses to open his pack a black dog appears and enquires of Alizon what should it do to him.

After some discussion she bids the dog lame the pedlar, whereupon Law falls down and is carried, bereft of speech, into an ale-house. Alizon and the dog follow him inside, stay a short while and then depart.

A letter sent to Halifax fulfils its purpose, for no sooner is the stricken man's son Abraham arrived in Colne than he fetches Alizon Device to his father's side. It is now the twenty-ninth day of March, eleven days after their first encounter, and John Law, his left side paralysed but his speech sufficiently returned, accuses the girl, in the presence of others, with having bewitched him.

Alizon confesses to it and begs forgiveness, which the pedlar grants. His son, however, is less charitable and one day later – on the thirtieth day of March – Abraham Law brings not only Alizon, but also her brother James and her mother Elizabeth before Roger Nowell Esquire, Magistrate, of Read Hall.

This incident was the pivot upon which turned the fate of the Pendle Witches, the breath of air that was needed to fan the dull glow of fear and suspicion into the fast-burning fuse of persecution, a transformation wherein Alizon Device was but the unwitting catalyst.

Who were they, then, these Pendle Witches? If one applies the title strictly, they were those witches – men and women – who infested the area of farming and hunting land known as Pendle Forest, and who were, together with sundry other witches from round about, brought to trial in August, sixteen-hundred and twelve, at Lancaster Assizes, for practising the devilish art of witchcraft.

At the heart of this Pendle brood were two families of witches – the Demdikes and the Chattoxes. Stemming from Old Mother Demdike (whose real name was Elizabeth Southerns) were: her son Christopher Howgate (whose different surname suggests either illegitimacy or his mother having been twice married), Elizabeth Device, the widow of John Device, and the issue of that union, James, Alizon and the child Jennet.

The family depending from Anne Whittle, otherwise known as Old Mother Chattox, was smaller, comprising only three names of significance – that of Chattox herself and those of her daughters Bessie and Anne, the latter being the wife of Thomas Redfearn.

That there were other local witches is a matter of fact, but it is with this ill-assorted brood – the Demdikes and the Chattoxes – that we are presently concerned. Making allowance for the element of bias and exaggeration implicit in the relevant seventeenth century records, we can be reasonably sure that, in the year of her arrest, Demdike was, like Chattox, old and decrepit, her sight almost gone. Each would be about eighty years of age, ill-shod and poorly fed and clothed despite their supposed great powers, yet still feared, the one haunting the byways of Pendle Forest on the arm of her elder granddaughter, the other constantly uttering gibberish, either from senility or in a splenetic endeavour to compound one curse upon another.

Demdike's daughter Elizabeth would probably be in her middle forties at this time and was undoubtedly an extremely ugly, not to say repulsive, woman, having one eye that was cast down and the other turned up – an affliction that had earned her the nickname of Squintin' Lizzie.

Elizabeth's son James was as sickly and weak-minded as his mother was ill-favoured and, although supposed to be a labourer, seems to have spent much of his time begging. Whether he was a little older or a little younger than his sister is difficult to determine, but Alizon would be in her late teens when she met John Law on the road to Colne, coming increasingly under Demdike's influence as she led the old woman from place to place.

Alizon's sister Jennet, a pert, precocious child of nine, was not adjudged a witch until twenty-one years later, when, in the year sixteen-hundred and thirty-three, there was a further outbreak of witchcraft in Lancashire.

Bessie Whittle escaped the stigma entirely; certainly she was not arrested and sent to Lancaster with the others, yet was apparently there the following year, presumably in connection with another matter.

And finally Anne Redfearn, Chattox's other daughter; Anne, who seems to have been a comely woman at one time, was arguably the most self-possessed and determined among those who stood trial at Lancaster Assizes, and it is perverse but perhaps understandable that, in an atmosphere so charged with the extremes and eccentricities of others, her part in things is the least well documented.

FAMILY TREES OF THE TWO MAIN WITCHES

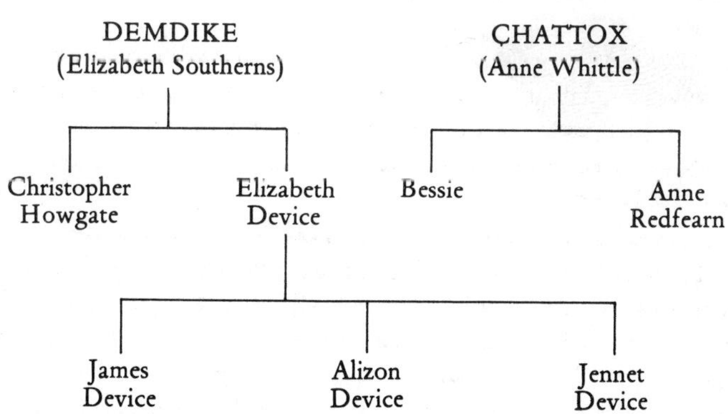

Magistrate Roger Nowell confronts three members of the Device family; Elizabeth, Alizon and James.

Part One: The Pendle Brood

Episode Two

Examination at Read Hall

It is yet the thirtieth day of March and Abraham Law has just caused three of the Pendle Witches, Alizon Device, her slow-witted brother James and her mother Elizabeth to appear at Read Hall.

Roger Nowell, one of the King's Justices in these parts, listens attentively as Alizon's story unfolds. She confesses freely to the incident on the road to Colne, departing in only one particular from the evidence presented against her, insisting that she sought to buy, not beg, some pins from the pedlar.

Then, impulsively, she tells how her grandmother, Demdike, had counselled her to adopt a familiar, or spirit, which if allowed to suck at her body would thereafter satisfy her wants and do her bidding. Thus is explained the presence of the black dog that molested John Law, Alizon having made her pact with it two years previously.

Next she relates how she led Demdike late at night to a sick cow belonging to John Nutter, who asked her to heal it, instead of which Demdike bewitched the beast unto death. How, on another occasion, when she, Alizon, brought some milk into the house part of it turned into butter without Demdike having touched it. How, sometime after she and her grandmother were ordered off the land of Richard Baldwin of Wheathead, she again accompanied Demdike late at night, following which excursion Baldwin's daughter became ill and eventually died.

The talkative Alizon leaves Nowell in no doubt that the curses she claims to have heard the old woman heap upon Baldwin were fully realised.

She goes on to tell of the feud that existed between Demdike and Chattox, recalling the time when Malkin Tower, where Demdike lived with her kin, was robbed of some oddments of clothing and a quantity of oatmeal. Shortly afterwards Alizon says she saw one of the Chattox clan – either Bessie Whittle or Anne Redfearn – wearing one of the missing items. John Device, Demdike's son-in-law, contrived to keep the peace between the two families by promising Chattox an annual gift of meal. When a few years later Device neglected his promise, he died, but not before he had attributed his malady to the hand of Chattox. Her hand or not, the die, so to speak, was cast and Chattox stood accused.

Alizon also recalls the death of Anthony Nutter's small daughter Anne. This was two years ago, she informs Nowell, and happened a few weeks after Chattox had seen her and Anne at Nutter's place and vowed to get even with one or the other for supposedly laughing at her.

Yet another victim, according to Alizon, was the son of John Moore of Higham. Moore had invited Chattox's enmity by accusing her of souring his ale. Shortly afterwards the boy became poorly, and Alizon declares that she saw Chattox holding his likeness in the form of a clay image – and this at a time when the child was already ill, an illness that subsequently proved fatal.

Alizon is specific in two other cases – that of Hugh Moore of Pendle, who died after charging Chattox with putting a spell on his cattle, and that of John Nutter whom Demdike had crossed concerning his sick cow. Nutter had given Chattox's daughter Elizabeth a dish of milk, over which her mother was muttering some incantation, when Nutter's son kicked at the dish and spilt the contents. A day later one of the John Nutter's cows died.

Not to be outdone, Alizon's brother James speaks up and denounces his own sister. According to James, someone called Henry Bulcock had recently called at Malkin Tower and accused Alizon of bewitching his child, whereupon she had admitted to the sin and begged Bulcock to forgive her.

What Alizon Device said at Read Hall provided Nowell with conclusive evidence of her own guilt and sufficient insight into the actions of others to warrant further enquiry.

Just why Alizon spoke so freely is open to conjecture. She was, perhaps, both gullible and articulate – and not a little frightened, a combination that, once the floodgates were open, compelled her to tell all. Then there was the magisterial presence of Nowell himself, a man skilled in the art of putting questions and assiduous in discharging the responsibilities of his office.

Bearing in mind both these factors and the substance and fabric of her surroundings, the psychological pressures on Alizon to confide must have been considerable. Conditioned as she was, it is not surprising that she acted as she did. Also, it must be remembered that there were three generations living together in squalid conditions at Malkin Tower and that it was Alizon's lot to lead the old Demdike about. We know from the girl's conduct at Colne, and her alleged conduct when Henry Bulcock confronted her, that she was of an emotional and impulsive nature. At home, under the dominance of Demdike, her emotions would be suppressed. Could it be that in the potent atmosphere of Read Hall she saw an opportunity of gaining her freedom and, on impulse, seized it?

In the event, she merely exchanged one prison for another, for at the end of the proceedings Elizabeth and James were allowed to depart, while Alizon remained in custody.

Demdike, when younger, encounters the boy Tibb in a quarry near Newchurch-in-Pendle.

Part One: The Pendle Brood

Episode Three

Examination at Fence

It is now three days later, the second day of April, and Demdike, Chattox and Anne Redfearn, together with sundry witnesses, are assembled at Ashlar House, Fence, there to be questioned by Roger Nowell.

Under Nowell's prompting, Demdike recalls that some twenty years ago, near a quarry in Goldshaw Booth, she came upon the Devil in the shape of a boy, his coat half black, half brown. The boy, whose name was Tibb, offered his allegiance in return for her soul. The bargain was struck and in later years Tibb appeared to Demdike variously as a black cat, a brown dog and a hare. The last time she saw him was during a quarrel with Richard Baldwin, when Tibb asked for and received her consent to visit harm upon the miller or his family.

Demdike went on to explain the art of destroying a person's life by making and hardening a clay picture of the intended victim, describing how to prick it with pins or thorns in that part to be injured, or if any part of the body were to be consumed how it could be brought about by taking that part of the image and burning it. Should the body be required to be consumed utterly, then the whole of the picture was burned.

Her own tale told, Demdike denounces Chattox and her daughter Anne, telling of the time when they were sitting by a ditch outside Anne's house making three pictures of clay. Tibb, in the guise of a black cat, identified these as being of the Nutters of Greenhead – Christopher, his son Robert and Robert's wife Marie. Inconsequentially, she adds that Tibb pushed her, Demdike, into the ditch for not joining in the enterprise.

Tibb emerges yet again in Demdike's rambling tale when, one Sunday morning as she sat nursing a child, he came to her in the form of a dog and sucked beneath her left arm. As a result of this, Demdike says she went out of her mind for eight weeks.

Now it is Chattox's turn, and she tells of *her* familiar, a spirit which first came to her some fifteen years ago in the form of a man called Fancie. She claims to have resisted him for about four years, which fixes their effective relationship from about the year sixteen-hundred and one. Chattox admits to using Fancie to bring harm to Robert Nutter of Greenhead after the young man had entered Anne Redfearn's house on his father's land and tried to seduce her. This was supposedly sometime around the year fifteen-hundred and ninety-five, presenting a discrepancy of five or six years between the date Fancie joined forces with Chattox and the time when he is alleged to have acted on her behalf.

But no-one present at Ashlar House comments, their minds no doubt dwelling morbidly on the fact that close upon the heels of Fancie's intervention Robert Nutter died, shortly to be joined by his father.

Robert's sister Margaret gives evidence of her brother's brush with Anne Redfearn and of his conviction that she had bewitched him. Next, the dead man's brother John recalls the time when Robert insisted that he was bewitched by both Anne *and* Chattox, pleading with his father to have them laid in Lancaster Castle.

Now Chattox resumes, informing the gathering of a charm she has for putting to rights soured milk. She claims to have applied it on behalf of John Moore's wife, and when the woman proved less than grateful, to have invoked Fancie who bit one of Moore's cows in the head, causing it to become first mad and then to die. Fancie was also instrumental in killing Anthony Nutter's cow, for no better reason than Chattox supposed Nutter to favour Demdike more than herself.

Demdike and Chattox are thus self-confessed witches, with Anne Redfearn implicated by association and the words of others, and it is only a formality for Roger Nowell to order their detention so that, in company with Alizon Device, they can subsequently be tried under the Witchcraft Act of sixteen-hundred and four.

Once again, with the exception of Anne Redfearn, the witches have spoken out, with the two old women vieing with one another as to who could tell most. Once again the psychological inducement to gossip – for that, in essence, is what the two old crones did – must have been intense, especially before such a receptive audience.

Notwithstanding the rough and ready ways of the period, and the harsh treatment meted out to those who fell foul of the law, it seems unlikely that physical methods were employed to extract the witches' confessions: there were too many witnesses present. The first hypothesis, therefore, remains the more likely. The same natural forces that worked against Alizon Device worked against Demdike and Chattox; in all three cases the urge to talk was made urgent.

Nowell himself would have been less than a man of his times if he had not been zealous in his examination at Fence, knowing as he did that his king – King James the first of England – entertained an implacable hatred of witches and was the author of a learned book on the subject, as well as being a staunch upholder of the notorious Witchcraft Act:

It is in the nature of things that Nowell would have prompted the defendants, encouraged witnesses, asking leading questions and interpreted to his own satisfaction the answers he received. Chattox was, from all accounts, incapable of coherent speech at any time; it is unlikely that, unless Nowell acted as her proxy, she could have overcome her impediment on this occasion.

Much of the evidence given at Fence concerned the witches' familiars and out of all those witches so far detained only Anne Redfearn appears not to have had one. We gather that Elizabeth Device did because when she was at Read Hall, Roger Nowell had her examined and was satisfied that he found its mark on her left side.

Nowell was nothing if not thorough in his dealings with the Pendle Witches and, as a consequence of his diligence, left his own mark.

Witches assembled at Malkin Tower, there to plot evil.

Part One: The Pendle Brood

Episode Four

The Great Assembly and Feast

It is noon on Good Friday, six days after the four witches had departed for Lancaster on the fourth day of April, and there are comings and goings at Malkin Tower. A great many witches converge on that place. The Devices are there – Elizabeth, James and young Jennet; Demdike's son, Christopher Howgate, is there with his wife; included in their vast number are Alice Nutter of Roughlee and Jennet Preston of Gisburn.

James Device is prominent at the meeting, having stolen a sheep from near the village of Barley the night before and added its carcase to the beef and bacon the witches feed on while they plan the release of the four women from Lancaster Castle, the blowing up of the castle itself and the murder of its gaoler, Thomas Covell. Another purpose of the meeting is to agree upon a name for Alizon Device's familiar and to lend support to Jennet Preston of Gisburn, who has just been released from the rigours of prison at York, acquitted of a charge of witchcraft brought by Thomas Lister, also of Gisburn.

The assembly and feast is the greatest expression of malice, in fact and intent, ever concentrated in one place, and the dire threats and terrible undertakings issuing therefrom strike at the well-being of all Christian men and women. They are present, these witches, to plot naught but evil. The power they wield is daunting. Nothing, it seems, can prevail against them.

This was the lurid picture painted for Roger Nowell and the Forest Constable, Henry Hargreaves, when news of the assembly of witches caused Nowell to order an investigation. That the investigation was conducted with great zeal is not in dispute; that the findings were, for the most part, fanciful is to understate the case.

A great throng at Malkin Tower? The place, notwithstanding its pretentious name, must have been little better than a hovel, probably overcrowded at the best of times. Feasting? Hardly that on a few scraps of beef and a hastily slaughtered sheep. The setting free of four of their kind from Lancaster Castle, the destruction of that place and the murder of its gaoler? Lancaster Castle was impregnable to the likes of them, and even if they could have got within its gates, Demdike and the others were doubtless in the sealed dungeon beneath the Well Tower. As for reaching the gaoler, the Malkin Witches had about as much chance of getting at him as they had of penetrating into the dungeon.

The business of choosing a name for Alizon's familiar had to be abandoned as, in the girl's absence, nothing could be concluded. It would be easy to be equally dismissive of the presence at Malkin Tower of Jennet Preston and Alice Nutter. Of the first, perhaps, but Mistress Nutter was a gentlewoman of good birth and standing living with her family at Roughlee Hall, and could have had little in common with a bunch of peasants. She could easily have been in the vicinity of Malkin Tower on legitimate business, and might even have spoken to one or other of the peasants about recent events, but more than that and credulity flies out the window.

But there were two witnesses ready to swear to Roger Nowell and his fellow magistrate Nicholas Bannister that Alice *was* at Malkin Tower and that she was privy to and took full part in what transpired there. And such witnesses! None other than James and Jennet Device, the one addle-brained, the other mischievous and attention-seeking, perfect foils for someone with sufficient motive for wishing Mistress Nutter seen where she was not.

As well as with the manifest nonsense concerning the so-called great assembly and feast, James Device regaled the magistrates with a long rigmarole about the manner in which he met his familiar, a dog called Dandie, and of hares that when not trying to pull him to pieces were lying on top of him at midnight or spitting fire at him as he walked about.

Nevertheless, evidence of a more concrete kind did emerge when James revealed that twelve years ago, at Newchurch, Chattox took three skulls from as many graves; also some teeth, keeping four of them and giving four to Demdike. Demdike's grisly share had remained hidden until dug up outside Malkin Tower by the Forest

Constable. As the find was at the instigation of James Device, the story attaching to it is suspect. On the other hand, it is possible that Chattox or Demdike, or both, did desecrate a grave, or graves, at sometime and that there was a degree of collaboration. Twelve years ago would put it at the very turn of the century, either just before or just after the clothing and meal were stolen from Malkin Tower. Either way, it is just tenable that the women were on terms, as the real feud between the two families did not commence until the death of John Device a few years later.

The Forest Constable unearthed the teeth – also a clay image – between Good Friday and the twenty-seventh day of April, because it was then that he handed over the investigation to the two magistrates. It was to them that James and Jennet Device told their wild stories about the assembly of witches and the rest of it, and it was to them that James owned up to two murders. The first after a Mistress Towneley of Carr Hall had accused him and his mother of stealing and slapped his back, whereafter Dandie, James's familiar, materialised and helped him fashion a picture of clay, which James dried and crumbled away during the course of a week. Two days hence Mistress Towneley died. On the second occasion, Dandie seems to have taken over entirely. When a man called Duckworth went back on his promise to give James a cast-off shirt, Dandie insisted that as James had actually touched Duckworth's person in some way, he, Dandie, had power over the man. Poor Duckworth, he was dead within the week!

James was equally ready to accuse his next of kin, telling Nowell how his mother and her familiar Ball had planned the death of a Barley man, one John Robinson, by making and crumbling a clay likeness. Sure enough, Robinson passed over only days after the three weeks it took Elizabeth Device to crumble his image.

At first Elizabeth denied the allegation, but later, when she learned that James and Jennet – her own children – had betrayed her, she broke down and confessed. She did more; she confirmed the identities of those present at Malkin Tower, but pleaded ignorance of all else that took place there save the intention of naming her daughter's familiar.

Once started, Elizabeth seems incapable of stopping and went on to admit to the disposal also of John Robinson's brother and, in collusion with Demdike and Alice Nutter, of a man she named as Henry Mitton of Roughlee.

Roger Nowell must have been well pleased with his day's work. Not only had he secured all the evidence he needed in order to proceed against some of the peasant witches, but, as a consequence of Elizabeth Device's admission concerning the man Mitton, he was now in a position to bring a capital charge against Mistress Nutter.

Elizabeth's contribution, coming as it did at the very end, could not have come better had it been contrived. Perhaps it had. Be that as it may, she and six others – James Device and his mother among them – were apprehended and despatched to join those already held in Lancaster Castle, leaving young Jennet Device alone on a darkening stage, her major role yet to come.

Part One: The Pendle Brood

Episode Five

Intermission at Lancaster Castle

It is the nineteenth day of May and Chattox is being questioned by the castle gaoler, Thomas Covell, assisted by the Mayor of Lancaster and a local justice of the peace. During the course of her interrogation, Chattox makes significant changes to the statement she made to Roger Nowell at Ashlar House on the second day of April.

Now she tells them that it was Demdike who introduced her to witchcraft and that the initiation took place at Malkin Tower, where their familiars, Tibb and Fancie, served them a meal. She says also that Demdike was responsible for the death of Richard Assheton of Downham, and was partially so in the case of Robert Nutter of Greenhead.

What prompted this change of heart? Was it simply because sometime between the fourth day of April and the nineteenth day of May Demdike had died in custody and Chattox thought to save her own life? If so, she certainly seems to have waxed eloquent. Altogether too eloquent, surely, for a woman given to incessant gibbering. This was not the first time Chattox had had a conveniently lucid interval when being questioned, and once again we are tempted to think that it was not what she actually said but what others wanted to hear, that was the common factor.

One possibility that would go far to explain the situation at Lancaster Castle is that when Demdike so thoughtlessly died, the officials there so wanted to damage her character as to make it seem that she had cheated the hangman rather than missed the opportunity of establishing her innocence. The distinction is a subtle one, but if this were the case, who better than Chattox to provide history with its verdict.

Wherever the truth lies, Chattox's second thoughts enabled Covell and the others to draw an even blacker line beneath Demdike's name than might otherwise have been possible.

Jennet Device giving evidence at Lancaster Assizes.

Part One: The Pendle Brood

Episode Six

Lancaster Assizes

It is Monday, the seventeenth day of August, and the Assizes of Oyer and Terminor (to hear and determine) are in session, presided over by Sir Edward Bromley and Sir James Altham, two of His Majesty's Judges.

It is here, too, that we first meet Thomas Potts, Clerk to this Court, among whose duties it is to take down in writing all that is heard and determined. No-one could be better suited to the task, for Master Potts is as anxious to find favour with his superiors as he is desirous of scourging the witches.

The first to be put up is Anne Whittle, alias Chattox, who is, following her altered testimony while in prison, charged with the single crime of bringing about the death of Robert Nutter of Greenhead. The old woman pleads not guilty, but the evidence mounts against her and she admits responsibility, throwing herself on the mercy of the court. She is contrite, she is humble, she even so far forgets her own troubles as to make an appeal on behalf of her daughter, Anne Redfearn.

Next on the Calendar is Elizabeth Device – Squintin' Lizzie – and all present are as much fascinated as repulsed by her grotesque appearance, for she both looks like a witch and sounds like one as she denies the murder by witchcraft of John Robinson of Barley, that of his brother James, and of complicity in the killing of Henry Mitton of Roughlee.

But Roger Nowell, who is prosecuting, plays his trump card when he calls young Jennet Device, Elizabeth's own daughter. Now the mother's fury knows no bounds and she becomes so violently abusive that she is taken out for a time. Meanwhile, Nowell stands Jennet on a table and she tells how, on one of his visits to Malkin Tower, Ball, her mother's familiar, entered into speech with Elizabeth and took orders from her to carry out the three murders.

Jennet's evidence, and the manner in which it is given, creates a strong impression on all present, and Roger Nowell adroitly adds

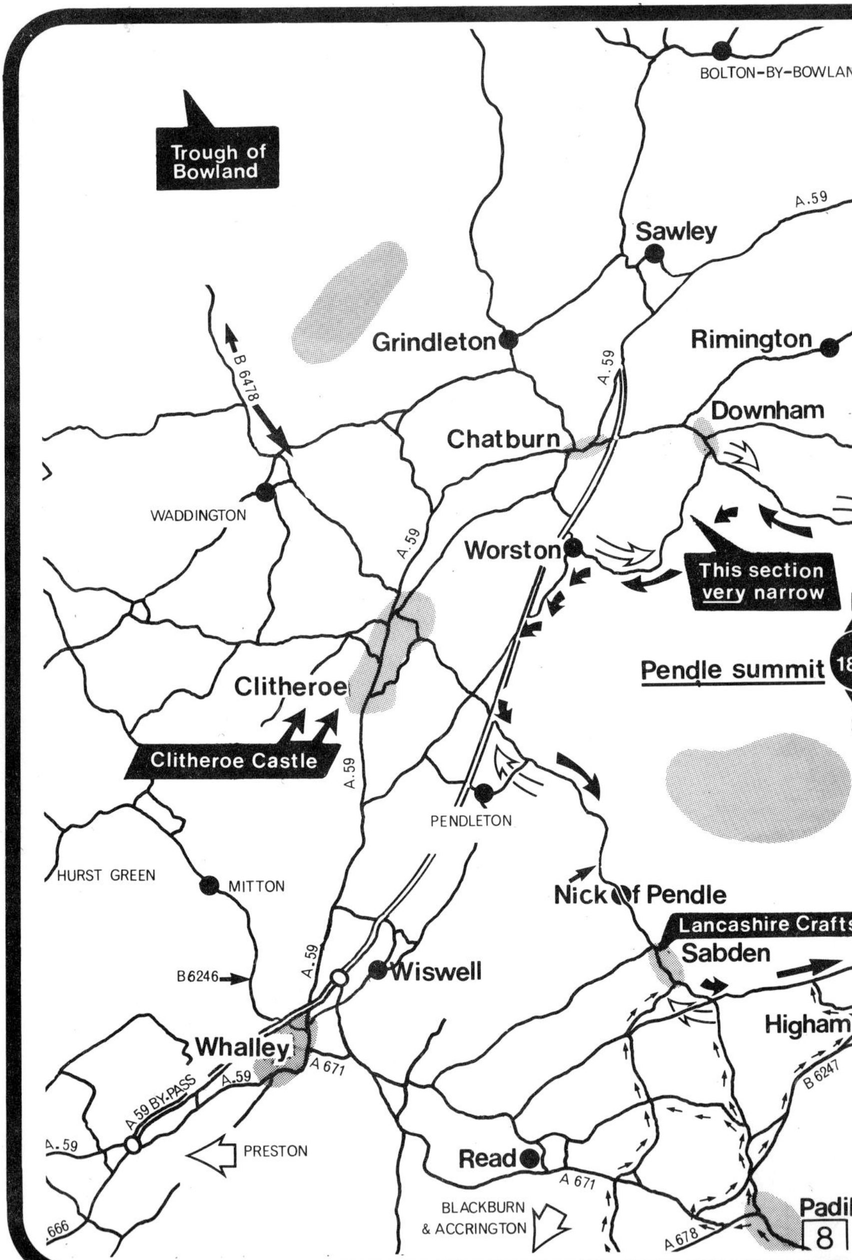

BOLTON-BY-BOWLAN
Trough of Bowland
A.59
Sawley
Grindleton
Rimington
B 6478
A.59
Downham
Chatburn
WADDINGTON
A.59
Worston
This section very narrow
Pendle summit
18
Clitheroe
Clitheroe Castle
A.59
PENDLETON
HURST GREEN
MITTON
Nick of Pendle
Lancashire Crafts
Sabden
A.59
B6246
Wiswell
Higham
Whalley
A 671
A.59
B 6247
A 59 BY-PASS
A.59
PRESTON
Read
A 671
BLACKBURN & ACCRINGTON
Padih
8
A 678
.666

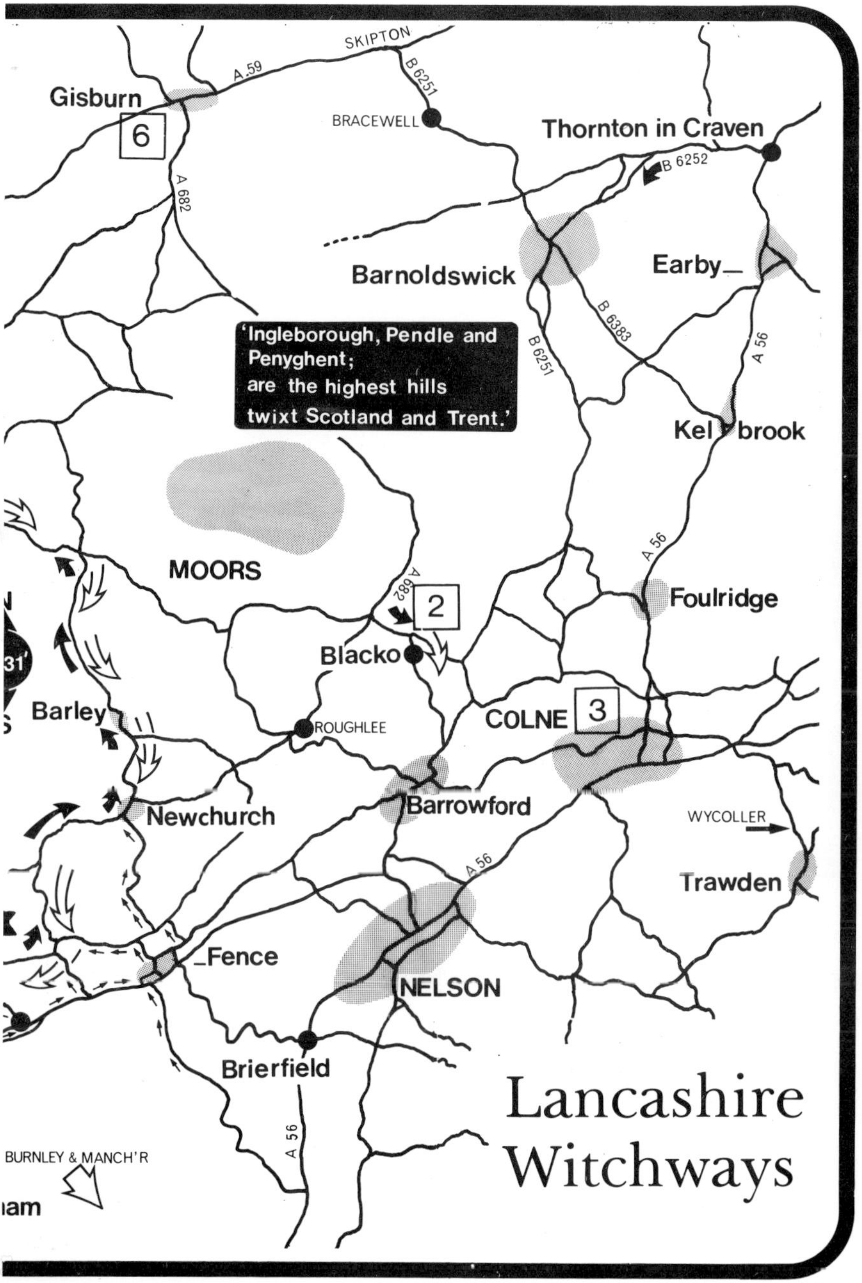

Lancashire Witchways

to it by introducing James's sworn statement naming his mother as hostess to the assembly of witches when they met on Good Friday.

When Elizabeth Device returns to the courtroom, she is at first defiant, but when she realises that, once more, her own children have conspired against her, her last shred of resistance ebbs away, leaving only her resigned plea for mercy to linger in its stead.

Elizabeth is followed into the dock by her son James, who is in such a state of collapse that he is supported where he stands. He is charged with two murders – those of Mistress Anne Towneley of Carr Hall and John Duckworth of Laund. James's intellectual and physical reserves are so far reduced that his responses are barely comprehensible as he acknowledges both crimes.

He is further charged with bewitching to death John and Blaze Hargreaves of Higham. This charge James refutes, but reckons without his sister, for Jennet's brief recall is sufficient to disqualify his denial. It was, she asserts, her brother's familiar, Dandie, who, acting on his behalf, took the lives of the two men.

At this point Sir Edward Bromley asks the jury to retire and consider their verdicts in respect of Anne Whittle (Chattox), Elizabeth Device and James Device. In each instance the finding is Guilty, and Master Potts' quill scratches busily in the Court Ledger.

And now Anne Redfearn. Self-contained, aloof almost, she denies and is found not guilty of the murder of Robert Nutter, only to be judged at fault in the death of his father Christopher. Chattox, already convicted, returns briefly to the courtroom and, taking all the blame attaching to Anne upon her own stooped shoulders, begs the judge to be merciful, while Anne, who has been constant throughout, maintains her innocence to the end.

If Anne's short trial has been something of an anti-climax to what went before, the next defendant brings the court to the height of expectancy. The public chatter is suddenly hushed, for Mistress Alice Nutter is no ordinary witch. Neither poor nor ignorant, nor without connections, she is a woman to be reckoned with, one who, should she choose, might take issue with Roger Nowell and best him. But it is not to be. For reasons known only to herself, Mistress Nutter remains silent – and forever an enigma.

Disdaining victory by default, Nowell yet again produces his key to locked doors. He arranges an identity parade, includes Alice Nutter in its number, and invites Jennet Device to pick out anyone who was present at Malkin Tower. Without hesitation she puts her hand into the hand of Mistress Nutter. Yes, the gesture proclaims in a manner more emphatic than words, this woman was at Malkin Tower!

There are no indignant denials, no histrionics; these two, so far removed in station and years, have linked hands and the clasp is, for Alice Nutter, as cold and binding as gyves and fetters. She is doomed, this strange woman, from that moment, yet remains impassive as she is adjudged guilty of the heinous crime of witchcraft. If the jury had been moved by Chattox's impassioned plea on behalf of her daughter, it was not so far moved as to be deflected from its stern duty. And if, in the case of Mistress Nutter, the jury was admiring of her dignified silence, it did not express its admiration in a tangible form. The verdicts were unequivocal. Anne Redfearn: Guilty. Alice Nutter: Guilty.

Finally to Alizon Device, she who met John Law on the road to Colne and so started all that was to follow. Alizon is not charged with murder, but with bringing about the injuries suffered by the pedlar when she cursed him on that fateful day in March.

Now, almost half a year later, John Law, his frame rigid and twisted, his head held at an unnatural angle and his speech much impaired, presents himself as witness for the prosecution. At the very sight of him, Alizon drops to her knees and confesses. Almost overcome by emotion, John Law confirms the charge and is emphatic concerning the presence of a black dog, describing its fearsome aspect when it followed him and the girl into the ale-house.

Alizon remains penitent, but declares herself as being unable to undo the damage the pedlar has suffered, whereupon the judge discharges him, undertaking to do something for his material welfare. Alizon Device's reward is equally swift: Guilty on her own confession. How Master Potts' pen races across the parchment.

The ink is hardly sanded before Potts is handing up his list of witches to Judge Bromley, who has them brought back to the bar for sentencing. The judge begins by reminding them of their good fortune in receiving such a fair trial, and of their debt to God for revealing their sins before it was too late for the redemption of their immortal souls. He ends by sentencing them to death by judicial hanging.

The Assizes give us our first glimpse of Master Thomas Potts, and the character that emerges is not unlike that of Uriah Heap. That he was God-fearing, deferential to his superiors and a fervent disciple of his king in his abhorrence of witches is patent, and it is to Potts that we owe almost all that is known about the Pendle Witches, for it is from his dusty writings that the story has come to us over the years. To that extent, it is fortunate that he was what he was – the diligent, prying little clerk of whom a contemporary might well have said: "Potts is the kind of man who knows his place and places his nose in the affairs of others."

It is with all these facets of Potts' character and personality in mind that we must look at his version of what happened at Lancaster Assizes. Chattox was again remarkably lucid, able even to make a moving appeal on behalf of her daughter. Coming as it did on top of her condemnation of Demdike in front of Thomas Covell and the two other examining officials on the nineteenth day of May, it appears that Chattox was cast in the twin mould of King's witness and fond mother.

If Chattox was moulded into her part, young Jennet Device, Demdike's granddaughter, was almost certainly groomed for and coached in hers. Jennet in a crowded court conducting herself with assurance; Jennet conversing with magistrates and officials; Jennet standing on a table talking away the life of her mother. Too pat. The maid needed neither prompting nor persuasion. She was word perfect. She was equally competent in the task of contradicting her brother's evidence concerning John and Blaze Hargreaves.

If one accepts the fact that Jennet was brain-washed, it is logical to take speculation a step further. After her mother and brother were arrested soon after Good Friday, someone needed to look after the child. Christopher Howgate, her uncle, *might* have done so; neighbours *may* have stepped into the breach. So might Roger Nowell Esquire, magistrate, of Read Hall. No-one knows where Jennet went or what became of her during those next critical weeks. Why should she not have ended up at Read, there in heady surroundings, fed on good food and flattery, to be primed for her part in coming events?

The trial of Anne Redfearn was at once a travesty and a contradiction in terms, in that she was acquitted of murdering someone against whom she had a grudge, and found guilty of doing away with a man with whom she had no quarrel. It was during Anne's trial that Chattox reappeared, making yet another lucid plea for her daughter's life. True or not, these interludes did two things – they made a refreshing change from the mutual spite and malice demonstrated by the Demdike brood, and at the same time shifted the mantle of greater evil from one matriarch to the other.

In regarding Mistress Alice Nutter, it might be said that, by keeping silent, she was her own worst enemy. That, however, would not be true. Somewhere or other, Alice had a much better enemy than herself. Once more Jennet Device was Roger Nowell's instrument in proving that Alice Nutter was at Malkin Tower on Good Friday. With what motive? There was some vague talk of a family plot to deprive Alice of her property; there is no evidence, as fiction has it, that at some time in the past she had bested Nowell in a court action over a boundary dispute.

And lastly, Alizon Device. It was fitting that things ended with whom they began. If Master Potts had had the ability and inclination to write the sort of blurb that appears on the dust jacket of a modern novel he might have said that it was with Alizon that the tale first started to flow . . . like water . . . like running water . . . like the water that flowed in the Lune hard by Lancaster Gaol. Instead, he left us a more pedestrian, if no less sinister, record, one in which Alizon was used from start to finish to bring about the downfall of herself and others. If this gullible, erratic girl did not actually knot the rope that the hangman used, she, with the help of Roger Nowell, assuredly plaited its threads.

Jennet Device places her hand into the hand of Jane Bulcock.

Part Two: Some Other Witches

Episode One

The Malkin Lot

One of the difficulties, even for the serious student, is in assimilating the names and deeds – or misdeeds – of all those other witches who were caught up in the events of sixteen-hundred and twelve. These lesser known witches outnumbered the sum of the Demdike and Chattox broods and it is a purpose of this present book to subtract the one lot from the other and to present separate calenders of those remaining witches who appeared at Lancaster Assizes, the exception being Jennet Preston who was tried at York.

As good a place to begin as any is at Malkin Tower on Good Friday, when some of these witches gathered at what came to be called the great assembly and feast. Not surprisingly, Roger Nowell and the Forest Constable were indebted, in the main, to James and Jennet Device for the names that follow: **Jane and John Bulcock**, of Moss End Farm, near Newchurch: mother and son, the Bulcocks were charged with bewitching Jennet Deane of Newfield Edge until she became sick and eventually mad. In court, young Jennet Device extended her hand in much the same fashion and in much the same circumstances as in the case of Alice Nutter, and Jane's fate was sealed. Jennet identified John Bulcock as the man who had attended the spit used for roasting the witches' meat. A nice touch this, giving her evidence just the right degree of home-spun authenticity. Although not arraigned on a capital charge, both Jane and John Bulcock were hanged.

Katherine Hewitt, of Colne, also known as Mouldheels: this woman was indicted for the killing, in concert with Alice Grey, of a child, Anne Foulds. James Device's statement to magistrates Nowell and Bannister, on the twenty-seventh day of April, made it clear that the two women had confessed to this at Malkin Tower on Good Friday. When, at the Assizes, Jennet Device touched Katherine Hewitt's hand in confirmation, Judge Bromley seems to have made a genuine attempt to test Jennet by introducing a ficticious name into the proceedings and asking her if this person also was at Malkin Tower. Perhaps Bromley considered her performance too good to be true. Whatever his thoughts, Jennet seems to have read them, for she evaded the trap and, in so doing, impressed the court with her apparent integrity. So much so that Katherine was found guilty, sentenced and hanged.

Alice Grey, also of Colne: this alleged witch was charged with being an accomplice of Katherine Hewitt in the murder of Anne Foulds, and of harbouring, with Hewitt, the intention of bringing harm to another child. At this point events take a more capricious turn than usual, for, although Master Potts' journal correctly links Grey with Hewitt, she is thereafter lumped with some Samlesbury witches, a different set of circumstances altogether. But fortuitous for Alice Grey, for she is acquitted and set free.

Jennet Preston, of Gisburn in Craven: Jennet's name remains prominent in events because it was she who, figuratively speaking, left prison at York one day and returned to it the next. After leaving the assembly and feast at Malkin Tower she was soon arrested and charged with the murder by witchcraft of Thomas Lister of Westby, near Gisburn, in the year sixteen-hundred and seven. Jennet's previous appearance at York had been in connection with the death of a child, but Judge Bromley found no fault with her. That was at the Lent Assizes of sixteen-hundred and twelve, shortly – and perhaps significantly – just before the Pendle witch-hunt had got under way and generated so much heat.

Certainly by the time Jennet Preston appeared at York a second time – this time before Judge Altham – the prosecution was better prepared. And why should it not be, for this time, on account of Jennet crossing the county boundary into Lancashire when she attended Malkin Tower, Roger Nowell had exercised his right to have her visited in Gisburn by Henry Hargreaves, the Forest Constable, and have statements taken.

James Device got in on the act, informing Nowell of Jennet's presence at Malkin Tower, of the assembly's promise to help her dispose of the present Thomas Lister, the son of Thomas Lister deceased, and of Jennet's departure on the back of her familiar, a white foal. Typical James Device nonsense, compounded by the fact that he claimed that the rest of the witches did likewise, their mounts being without. Just as well; there could not have been much room within!

▲ *Some of the Pendle Witches, as enacted in a BBC documentary film.*

The tower and porch of Colne Parish Church. The stocks are seen bottom left. ▲

A closer view. It was near Colne that Alizon Device cursed John Law. ▶

▲ *Horse shoes still hang there. It is said that hung thus, with the open end downwards, the luck escapes.*

◀ *Bull Hole Farm, where Demdike failed to cure an ailing cow.*

▲ *Pendle Hall Farm, whereabouts Chattox probably lived.*

The Main Gate of Lancaster Castle, wherein may be seen the court where the witches were tried. ▶

▼ *Bulcock's Farm, home of Jane and John Bulcock, both of whom were hanged as witches.*

▲ *Judges Lodgings, Lancaster. The castle lies a short distance above and behind.*

Another scene from the BBC film of the Pendle Witches. ▶

▲ *Fragment of a charm against witchcraft discovered at Foulridge, near Colne. The date is probably 17th century.*

◀ *The Covell Brass: memorial to Thomas Covell, prison governor, Lancaster Castle.*

▲ *The Ribblesdale Arms, Gisburn, originally built as a house for the Lister family who figured in the life (and death) of Jennet Preston, the Gisburn witch.*

▲ *Brass plaque to John Webster, in Clitheroe Church. Webster was the astute vicar of Kildwick who saw through the Edmund Robinson witch hunt in 1633.*

▲ *Downham, one of Lancashire's most beautiful villages, with Pendle Hill rising in the background. Richard Assheton, one of Demdike's alleged victims, lived here.*

◀ *Gawthorpe Hall, Padiham, home of Richard Shuttleworth, one of the magistrates who examined Edmund Robinson in 1633.*

▲ *Witches Galore! Shop at Newchurch-in-Pendle, just above the church where Chattox and Demdike were alleged to have robbed graves, and where witches are said to be buried.*

With Roger Nowell providing evidence from just across the way and Magistrate Thomas Heber of Marton, whose daughter was married to the reigning Thomas Lister, actively presenting it before. Judge Altham at York, Jennet Preston really stood very little chance second time round. She was heard on the twenty-seventh day of July, found guilty, and hanged two days later, thus preceding her Malkin friends presently in the dungeons of Lancaster Castle by a day over three weeks. With Jennet out of the way, the Lister family continued to prosper, building a fine house (now the Ribblesdale Arms) in the centre of Gisburn.

Having resurrected the bare bones of these Malkin Witches and put a little flesh on them, it only remains to re-inter them in the right place, at the right time and in the right company. All those named were at Malkin Tower on Good Friday and were arrested and sent to Lancaster. There, with the exceptions of Jennet Preston (who was tried at York) and Alice Grey (who was tried with the Samlesbury Witches), they were tried, sentenced and hanged along with Chattox and the rest.

Katherine Hewitt and the two Bulcocks – Jane and John – were heard between the hearings of Alice Nutter and Alizon Device. Katherine was found guilty at the same time as the jury delivered its verdict on Anne Redfearn and Alice Nutter, the Bulcocks – mother and son – receiving their verdict when Alizon Device suffered hers.

All in all, the time taken to deal with these miserable wretches, whom for the sake of convenience we have called the Pendle Witches and the Malkin Witches, was just three days – from the eighteenth day of August, when the Assizes began, to the twentieth day of the month, when the hangman earned his fee and the crowd waiting by the gallows sated its appetite.

Part Two: Some Other Witches

Episode Two

The Samlesbury Trio

Concurrent with the trials of the Pendle Witches and the Malkin Witches were those attaching to the Samlesbury Witches, from whose number is subtracted the name of Alice Grey (see previous episode: the Malkin Lot). The seven remaining are Jennet and Ellen Bierley, Jane Southworth, Isabell Sidegraves, Elizabeth Astley, John Ramsden and Lawrence Haye. Ramsden, Haye, Sidegraves and Astley we can dispense with, for they were quickly acquitted and bound over to be of good report at the next Assizes.

Two of the three remaining, Jennet Bierley and Ellen Bierley, were grandmother and aunt, respectively, to a girl in her early teens, Grace Sowerbutts, and were charged, together with Jane Southworth, with bewitching the girl. In this case the victim was also witness for the prosecution and, after identifying the accused in court, went on to tell of her experiences. First: she had seen her grandmother, Jennet Bierley, turn herself into a speaking dog, one that walked upright and encouraged her, Grace, to commit suicide by drowning. When she failed to comply, the same dog visited certain unpleasantries upon her. Second: the two women had taken her at night to a house in Samlesbury where the older woman took a child from its bed and introduced a nail into its navel in order to suck its blood. When, some time subsequently, the child died, the same pair, witnessed by Grace, snatched its body from a fresh grave and later ate it. The bones, they made into a sort of stock, the fat from which could be used as a magic cream to change the user into another form. Third: the two Bierley women, Jane Southworth and herself had enjoyed regular assignations, at a place known as Red Bank across the River Ribble, with four black things, like men except in the face, with whom they danced and had intercourse.

At this point the accused women demanded of Judge Bromley that he probe Grace Sowerbutts' conscience so that she might confess who had persuaded her to commit perjury. Surprisingly, the girl's confidence evaporated to the extent of admitting to such a grey eminence in the substance of Christopher Southworth – related to

Jane Southworth, one of the accused – who seems to have harboured a grudge against all three women for renouncing the church of Rome. The master had, however, prepared the pupil badly. According to her the three women did not have spirits, or familiars, but themselves changed into another form; in the second place, the black things they consorted with on the banks of the Ribble were topsy-turvy; it was the Devil's feet – the cloven hoofs – that were different to the feet of men, not his countenance. So Southworth and his witness had got it all wrong and it was no less an authority than Master Potts who pointed out these matters after Judge Bromley had ordered Grace Sowerbutts to be examined by an independent magistrate. The outcome was a complete retraction of all she had claimed, placing the perjury totally where it belonged. As a consequence, Jennet Bierley, Ellen Bierley and Jane Southworth were discharged.

At any other time it is probable that the charges would never have been brought in the first place, not even in the circumstances then prevailing in the England of James the First. But times were not normal. Not far to the east the Pendle Witches and the Malkin Witches had been sought out and apprehended, the Gisburn Witch had been returned to the place from whence she came, Nowell and Bannister were making a name for themselves. Is it to be wondered at if Robert Holden, the Samlesbury magistrate, found such excitement contagious.

Chronologically, there are indications that this was so in as much as it was not until the fifteenth-day of April that Holden took evidence in respect of the Samlesbury Witches, eleven days after Demdike, Chattox and the others had been despatched to Lancaster, and five days after the meeting at Malkin Tower on Good Friday. However, Holden got his witches to the Castle in good time for the Assizes, and the case was heard on the morning of the nineteenth day of August, between the time on the eighteenth day, when Anne Redfearn was acquitted on one charge, and the day following when she was found guilty on a second.

So much for the Samlesbury trio. With that sort of track record, it is understandable that Robert Holden appears to have faded into the rural background from which he so briefly – and embarrassingly – emerged, no doubt thereafter confining his hunting instincts to game of a different kind.

Part Two: Some Other Witches

Episode Three

Two more witches

The Padiham Witch: with the appearance and sentence of Alizon Device, chronologically the last in line of all the witches thus far tried, Roger Nowell's proprietary interest in the Summer Assizes ceased. Alizon was followed by Margaret Pearson of Padiham, and the evidence presented against her was a matter for Nowell's colleague, Nicholas Bannister.

Margaret was no stranger to the courts, for this was her third known appearance, the offences, on the face of it, diminishing in seriousness, from murder the first time, to bewitching a neighbour on the second occasion, and now on account of doing away with a mare belonging to a man called Dodgson.

It was Margaret Pearson's misfortune to share her captivity with Chattox, for it was not long after her own sentence that that old chatterbox is up to her regular game of character assassination. She had already done a hatchet job in the case of Demdike and attempted another one in respect of Pearson. Indeed, she bestowed the ultimate in accolades when she told her interrogators that not only was the accused a very wicked woman, she was undoubtedly as wicked as herself. There was, as they say, no answer to that, and Chattox seems to have had a field day. Nothing was too far-fetched: Margaret Pearson's familiar was a cloven-footed man; she had disposed of Dodgson's mare by invading its stable and sitting on it until it expired; what is more she had confided to Chattox that she had murdered two of the Childers family – mother and daughter.

Powerful stuff, yet Nicholas Bannister chose one Jennet Booth's testimony as being the more damaging. While Booth was carding wool in Pearson's house in Padiham, a toad – or something like a toad – jumped out of a smouldering fire and had to be removed by means of tongs. A classical "so what?" situation one would have thought, for if a toad, or any other creature, pops into a hot hearth, it is likely to pop right out again. But Bannister was right, the court was impressed – a toad was nothing if not sinister. The jury found the Padiham witch guilty and the judge sentenced her to stand in the pillory at Clitheroe, Lancaster, Padiham and Whalley, and then to serve a one year's term of imprisonment.

To say that Margaret Pearson thus came off better than those who went to the gallows is to fail to appreciate the ordeal of the public pillory, the weary body and mind-sapping journeys from one place of humilation to another, only to be followed by the unrelieved misery and degradation of what dramatic novelists used to call durance vile. Perhaps it was the other witches – those who hanged – who got off lightly. After all, theirs was but a suspended sentence!

The witch from Widnes: this so-called witch did not live in or about Pendleside; was not at the meeting at Malkin Tower; did not consort with Demdike, Chattox and the rest, yet found herself hauled from her home near St. Helens and sent to Lancaster, there to be tried at the Summer Assizes.

Other than the expressed grievances of a young man who claimed that Isobel Roby had occasioned him aches and pains, no specific charge is recorded in Master Thomas Potts' writings; instead, there is a vague, unfinished reference to her . . . *having made use of her devilish and wicked arts.* In plural!

Not much, but sufficient for the jury to return a verdict of guilty, for the same legislation that enabled a suspect to be tried for almost anything left precious few loopholes through which a witch might slip. In Isobel Roby's case the hole was the loop the hangman made on Thursday the twentieth day of August.

The witch Frances Dickinson on her magic steed.

Part Three: The Outbreak of 1633

Episode One

Hoarstones

It is the first day of November in the year sixteen-hundred and thirty-three, twenty one years and three months after the memorable Summer Assizes at Lancaster, and an eleven year old boy, Edmund Robinson of Wheatley Lane, is out that night picking wild fruit when he meets two greyhounds, one black and one brown, which he grasps by the strings depending from their collars.

When confronted by a hare, neither dog reacts and the boy beats them with a stick, whereupon the black dog changes into a woman known to Edmund as Frances Dickinson, and the brown dog into a boy. Frances offers Edmund a shilling to keep quiet, but he refuses the bribe, saying he will report her as a witch. Meanwhile the other boy has changed into a white horse upon which the woman places a bridle and, mounting, forces Edmund Robinson to do likewise. They then ride to a large house in Wheatley Lane, known as Hoarstones, where Edmund sees men and women feasting off lumps of butter and flesh pulled from above into basins by means of ropes. He also sees three women recover three clay pictures stuck with thorns.

Fearful of the outcome the boy flees and, although chased by two witches, manages to make good his escape when his pursuers are scared off by a lone rider near a place called Boggart Hole.

Thus, after a pause of twenty-one years, the touchpaper of yet another witch-hunt is kindled into smouldering life, this time by a boy not much older than was Jennet Device when she did so much to further the aims of Roger Nowell in the witch trials of sixteen-hundred and twelve. This time the examining magistrates were John Starkie of Huntroyd and Richard Shuttleworth of Gawthorpe, who waited three months before taking statements from Edmund Robinson and his father. Neither magistrate seems to have been any more critical of the evidence than was Nowell of his informants twenty-one years earlier.

The credibility gaps gape like yawning pelicans. It was night time – in Novemeber – when the boy claimed to have met the two greyhounds, one black, the other brown. What exceptional eyesight to have been able to discern, let alone differentiate between, two such sombre hues. And how significant that the dogs should be the colour they were. A cynic might conclude that the choice was not so much natural as inspired by the story of Demdike's familiar Tibb, who materialised from a boy dressed in a coat half black and half brown.

The presence of the unknown boy who first emerged out of the brown greyhound and then changed into a white horse is thus the Demdike phenomenon in reverse order, the elaboration of the white horse presumably being necessary to transport everyone to Hoarstones in time to see the witches performing their version of the Indian Rope Trick. Young Robinson must have been fascinated to watch them pulling down butter and meat from the rafters by means of ropes; just how butter was tethered in this way and jerked down so accurately into waiting basins is not explained.

Equally mysterious – and unlikely – was the earlier presence of a hare, which seems to have excited Edmund more than the two greyhounds; so much so that he beat them with a stick he happened to be carrying. Well, where there is one hare there is frequently another, and it is not without logic to associate Edmund's hare – at least in his own mind and in the tale he had to tell – with the hare that lay on top of James Device. Or the one that wrestled with him. Or the one that spat fire. These imaginings would have entered into the cupboard of local gossip, hearsay and superstition, and if the introduction, however irrelevant, of a hare into a later scenario would add to its drama, then the cupboard was there to be raided.

Then there is the matter of the feasting witches. Over the years the feast at Hoarstones has become confused with the so-called great assembly and feast of witches at Malkin Tower. The one is not the other, but the two are so alike as to consign the whole of Edmund Robinson's evidence irretrievably into the copy-category.

One would have thought that, faced with such an obvious ploy, magistrates Starkie and Shuttleworth would have viewed at least this part of Robinson's story with scepticism. Instead, they swallowed it whole, influenced, no doubt, by Starkie who, as a boy had been possessed by demons. Consequently, he would have listened credulously to accusations concerning witches and witchcraft made by another boy. It was a case of boy talking to boy. Starkie believed in demoniacle possession and would have accepted hallucination as real. But the point is academic, for Edmund Robinson was neither possessed nor hallucinating; he was telling lies.

Part Three: The Outbreak of 1633

Episode Two

Lancaster and London

It is sometime following the tenth day of February, in the year sixteen-hundred and thirty-four, and no less than seventeen of the Hoarstones Witches languish in Lancaster Castle – Jennet Device, woman of the child whose kin had been hanged almost twenty-two years before – among them. Each is tried and found guilty, but sentence is stayed pending the outcome of deliberations in London undertaken by the King (now Charles the First) and his Privy Council.

Time passes and before a report on the women by the Bishop of Chester can be prepared, four of their number – Jennet Hargreaves, Mary Spencer, Frances Dickinson and Margaret Johnson are despatched to London, located in the Ship Tavern in Greenwich, and examined by representatives of the medical profession and by King Charles.

More time passes – agonisingly slowly – during which the London four are made the objects of public spectacle; they are displayed at the Fleet Prison; plays about them are published and enacted before avid audiences, and it is not until the second day of July, in the year sixteen-hundred and thirty-five, that the medical panel declares them free from any morbid sign or mark. Declared free, but not freed. The distinction is a cruel one, for these women and their sisters in Lancaster Castle are to remain in captivity for a long time.

———

Meanwhile, Edmund Robinson and his father, also called Edmund, were putting their time to better – and more profitable – use as witch-finders. Robinson senior and another man, young Edmund's uncle, exploited the boy by parading him round various churches in the locality, where he declared random members of the congregation to be witches. But the curate at Kildwick in Craven, John Webster, was an astute man who, following a witch-finding charade at his own church, went to the house where Edmund Robinson was staying with his father and uncle and demanded to know if he had told the truth, or otherwise, concerning the alleged gathering of witches at Hoarstones.

Understandably in the circumstances, the two men prevented the boy from answering. If nothing else, they had their new-found livelihood to protect. It is known that prior to his son becoming a celebrity, Robinson was a poor man and that he had since become more affluent. Clearly he and his henchman had going what would nowadays be called an extortion-cum-protection racket – the more victims they could direct the boy to denounce as witches, the greater were their chances of blackmailing others into paying exemption money.

Shortly after Webster's intervention, the trio were called to London and there subjected to the elementary technique of being separated and questioned in isolation. Young Edmund promptly spilled the beans, admitting that the entire sequence of supposed events was a fiction engineered by his father and his uncle. This rings true; the boy obviously had a fertile imagination and a glib tongue, but he needed the assistance of more mature minds to realise his talents.

And that appears to have been that, for notwithstanding that this retraction took place in the year sixteen-hundred and thirty-four, it was not followed by pardon and release for the seventeen women then in prison. On the contrary, they were still there several years later.

As for the architects of their plight – the two Edmunds and the shadowy uncle – the two older frauds simply dropped out of sight. Whether they remained in custody, went back home or lived their lives out elsewhere remains a mystery. Only the boy seems to have emerged positively, returning to live in Wheatley Lane. The last we hear of him is as a man of fifty-two, then known as Ned o' Roughs and given to telling of his youthful escapades. Boys would be boys, it seems, even in those days.

Chattox fashioning a picture of clay on the banks of Pendle Water.

Part Four: Post Mortem

Clearly the Pendle Witches were not witches at all, but a group of ignorant peasants scraping a living by begging and stealing from those better off than themselves. Equally clearly they half believed that they *were* witches, or, at least, that they had certain powers to harm or to heal, and that they were associated with bonded demons, or familiars.

There must have been a lot of stray animals scavenging the countryside in those days and it follows that a few of these would form an itinerant attachment to those human beings in a similar plight to themselves, sheltering from time to time in their hovels, snatching a scrap of food from hearth or table. It is but a short step to build up these lean predatory creatures into manifestations of the Devil. And if, as no doubt was the case, a dog or a cat, following its human counterpart about, was present when something a little odd occurred, then it is a shorter step still to attribute the abberation to one or the other, or both.

This does not account for the more bizarre examples, such as when James Device claimed to have fought with hares and so on, but James was, perhaps, a special case. If his condition were to be diagnosed today, it is probable that he would be found to be suffering from schizophrenia, in which case he may very well have seen hares and, indeed, felt himself to be persecuted by them. Certainly, his behaviour throughout was pathological.

Much, too, was made of witches' marks – marks and places on the so-called witches bodies at which their familiars drew sustenance. Devil's marks also – growths and appendages said to erupt when the witches made their covenant with the Devil. But it must be remembered that this was the seventeenth century, when warts and nodules and supernummery nipples and the like would have to be endured. How logical that, in the superstitious climate of the times, these deformities, large and small, would excite the morbid fancy of those more fortunate or not required to reveal their own blemishes. And what of the witches themselves? What did they think? Some of their marks might have appeared after the arrival of a particular dog or cat. An open sore perhaps. What more likely that an animal with a depraved appetite should lick at it and thereafter be associated with it.

Then there is the matter of curses and cures. Of course these peasants cursed. They were beggars, social outcasts. Cursing was their only means of positive expression when wronged or slighted. And if, following such a curse, a man or a child or a beast fell sick it was all too easy to draw the conclusion that the two events were connected. After all, there was a great deal of sickness in those days and a particularly high rate of infant mortality. If, on the other hand, the victim recovered and one of the witches was in the vicinity, then it was supposed that the curse had been removed and a cure effected.

Sometimes, no doubt, the cure would be genuine. Demdike and Chattox especially would be wise in the ways of herbs and potions and would on occasion be called upon to ease the condition of a sickly cow or sheep. That they muttered incantations over their specifics was so much mumbo-jumbo. It is significant in this context that they never had much luck in remedying soured ale; there was no more a cure for that then as there is today!

It is interesting at this point to so far digress as to consider the lump of butter said to have materialised spontaneously in a piggin of blue milk. It is likely that the milk was carried some distance to Malkin Tower and that it was considerably slopped about in its progress. So much agitated that there was a trace of butter at the end of the journey? Just possible, even if we do take blue milk to mean milk with precious little body in it.

When not out begging, the witches spent much of their time in idleness, and it is small wonder that they found time to fashion their dreaded pictures of clay. These evil little masterpieces relied totally for their effect on the power of suggestion. Demdike and the others were convinced that by making an image of their intended victim and then mutilating it, the subject would become ill or perish. But that part of the equation was necessary only for the witches' own satisfaction. What really mattered, indeed the only thing that mattered, was that the victim believed in the outcome. Under those circumstances, it is acceptable that illness – even death – could, and did arise. But the victim would have to *know,* and to this end the fact that the images were fashioned in public, as it were, would ensure that bad news travelled fast.

But prevention is better than cure, and where there are witches, there is witchbane, a means of warding off their evil powers. This might take the form of a plant or talisman, some article that, through usuage, was regarded as magic. The bane of the Pendle Witches might, more pointedly, be said to have taken the form of two men of widely different background and calling – John Law, pedlar, of Halifax and Roger Nowell, gentleman, magistrate and landowner, of Read Hall.

Law could not have been more appropriately named, for it was he who, through his son, caused the witches to fall foul of the magistrate. There is little doubt that what overtook the pedlar on the road to Colne was not a curse, but a stroke. He was of that build, of that age, burdened by a heavy pack and enraged at being importuned by Alizon Device and her mangy camp follower.

But one man's stroke of misfortune is another man's stroke of luck, and the outcome was that Roger Nowell was able to get his teeth into a matter close to the heart of his king and bring it to a triumphant conclusion.

If the comments directed towards Roger Nowell seem acute, it is because it is time his part in things was looked at with a fresh eye. Of all those who took part in the drama that unfolded during the spring and summer of the year sixteen-hundred and twelve, only Nowell had the time, opportunity and motive to manipulate the truth and coach his star witness; only Nowell stood to gain from the outcome, not materially but in prestige and status. No-one else fills the bill. Not the witches themselves, they were too ignorant. Not their neighbours, the yeoman farmers and millers, they were too busy earning a living. Not Master Thomas Potts, clerk and chronicler, he only came into it at the Assizes. It had to be someone with time to spare and power to act – someone like Nowell.

If so, it would appear that this single-minded man won the day totally. And yet, in her own way, Demdike scooped him, for not only did she anticipate the hangman, she bequeathed a mystery that remains unsolved to this day – the site of her home, Malkin Tower. Was it at Saddler's field, near Newchurch, a spot in close juxtaposition with those other locations cropping up in the vicinity of Pendle Forest – Greenhead, Roughlee, Fence, Barley? The logic is persuasive; regular sightings in these parts, age and infirmity militating against a farther-flung habitation. Or was it at a place near Blacko, off the road 'twixt Gisburn and Colne?

The one possibility does not preclude the other, for in those days folk trudged miles, whether begging or merely wandering. Perhaps the truth lies in both camps. Could it be that Demdike's life began in one place and ended, short of Lancaster Castle, in another? We may never know, any more that we shall know the origin of the name Malkin Tower. Was it derived from *Malt Kiln*? From *Mal Kin,* an educated, and therefore unlikely, swipe at Demdike's progeny? Was it connected with the *Malkins* – hares – that *toured* the fields thereabouts? Or was it simply a derisive description of a slum?

Today, out of all those witches who peopled the purlieus of Pendle Forest and beyond, only three spring readily to the popular mind: Demdike, Chattox and Alice Nutter. Master Thomas Potts cast the first two in leading roles, and later writers enhanced their status, also Mistress Nutter's, who features prominently in Robert Neill's best-selling romance *Mist Over Pendle.* Two additional factors have combined to keep Alice's name in the public eye – the continued existence, albeit much changed in purpose, of her home, Roughlee Hall, and the so-called witch's grave at Newchurch. Here, in the churchyard, hard by the church itself, is the family grave of the Nutters, and although Alice Nutter's name does not appear on the headstone superstition has it that she is buried there. This is almost certainly not so, but it helps keep the legend alive and adds to its charisma.

Of the other witches, just a few flit, half-remembered, across the latter-day stage: Elizabeth Device; Alizon; Jennet Device – once as a child and, later, as the victim of one; Anne Redfearn; Jennet Preston, the Gisburn Witch; Frances Dickinson; and possibly, just possibly, one or two more. Beyond these, the rest are more shadowy still, which is a pity, because they were no less real, just as much sinned against and equally deserving of our attention.

Hopefully, the technique we have adopted in presenting them in this book, the creation of faction rather than fiction and the separating of the women into close-knit groups might render them, if not any more endearing, at least – more familiar!